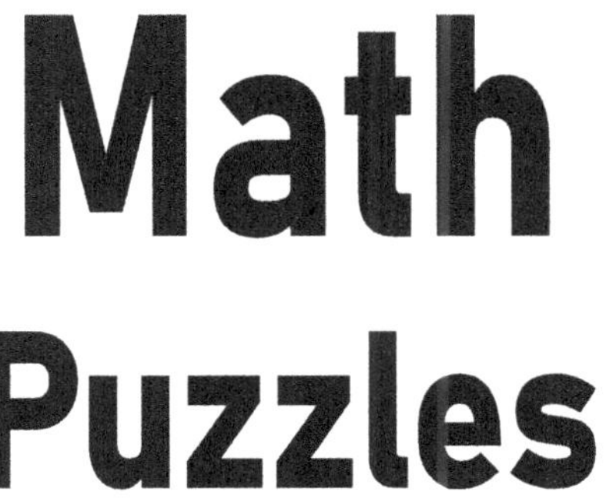

Math Puzzles

This Book Belongs To :

Lucy spencer

Table of contents

Across -Downs

Fill in the empty boxes with numbers in order to solve the operations both horizontally and vertically.

5	+	35	+	70	=		◀ 110
+		+		+		+	
75	+	5	+	1	=		◀ 81
+		+		+		+	
68	+	48	+	97	=		◀ 213
=		=		=		=	
	+		+		=		◀ 404
▲ 148		▲ 88		▲ 168			

HORIZONTALLY

5 + 35 + 70 = 110

75 + 5 + 1 = 81

68 + 48 + 97 = 213

148 + 88 + 168 = 404

VERTICALLY

5 + 75 + 68 = 148

35 + 5 + 48 = 88

70 + 1 + 97 = 168

110 + 81 + 213 = 404

Across Downs

1.

305	-	288	+	326	=	
-		+		-		+
288	+	960	-	95	=	
+		-		+		+
752	-	185	+	910	=	
=		=		=		=
	+		+		=	

Across Downs

2.

314	-	200	+	749	=	
-		+		-		+
200	+	339	-	30	=	
+		-		+		+
954	-	186	+	183	=	
=		=		=		=
	+		+		=	

3.

379	-	155	+	166	=	
-		+		-		+
155	+	594	-	86	=	
+		-		+		+
250	-	223	+	445	=	
=		=		=		=
	+		+		=	

Across Downs

4.

222	-	38	+	303	=	
-		+		-		+
38	+	995	-	52	=	
+		-		+		+
457	-	291	+	542	=	
=		=		=		=
	+		+		=	

Across Downs

5.

168	-	75	+	427	=	
-		+		-		+
75	+	372	-	325	=	
+		-		+		+
705	-	137	+	829	=	
=		=		=		=
	+		+		=	

6.

91	-	54	+	586	=	
-		+		-		+
54	+	429	-	418	=	
+		-		+		+
271	-	65	+	368	=	
=		=		=		=
	+		+		=	

Across Downs

7.

628	-	160	+	257	=	
-		+		-		+
160	+	111	-	15	=	
+		-		+		+
134	-	50	+	56	=	
=		=		=		=
	+		+		=	

8.

52	-	46	+	739	=	
-		+		-		+
46	+	120	-	54	=	
+		-		+		+
251	-	90	+	857	=	
=		=		=		=
	+		+		=	

9.

999	-	208	+	172	=	
-		+		-		+
208	+	643	-	91	=	
+		-		+		+
177	-	56	+	674	=	
=		=		=		=
	+		+		=	

Across Downs

10.

41	-	14	+	503	=	
-		+		-		+
14	+	925	-	335	=	
+		-		+		+
462	-	219	+	951	=	
=		=		=		=
	+		+		=	

Across Downs

11.

932	-	871	+	367	=	
-		+		-		+
871	+	914	-	74	=	
+		-		+		+
525	-	217	+	35	=	
=		=		=		=
	+		+		=	

Across Downs

12.

993	-	370	+	320	=	
-		+		-		+
370	+	991	-	310	=	
+		-		+		+
246	-	94	+	840	=	
=		=		=		=
	+		+		=	

13.

845	-	616	+	429	=	
-		+		-		+
616	+	765	-	43	=	
+		-		+		+
595	-	500	+	451	=	
=		=		=		=
	+		+		=	

14.

943	-	550	+	71	=	
-		+		-		+
550	+	792	-	45	=	
+		-		+		+
525	-	206	+	589	=	
=		=		=		=
	+		+		=	

15.

408	-	322	+	188	=	
-		+		-		+
322	+	515	-	167	=	
+		-		+		+
827	-	339	+	475	=	
=		=		=		=
	+		+		=	

16.

794	-	110	+	649	=	
-		+		-		+
110	+	156	-	134	=	
+		-		+		+
320	-	111	+	795	=	
=		=		=		=
	+		+		=	

17.

957	-	635	+	80	=	
-		+		-		+
635	+	935	-	3	=	
+		-		+		+
708	-	604	+	338	=	
=		=		=		=
	+		+		=	

18.

95	-	88	+	971	=	
-		+		-		+
88	+	616	-	281	=	
+		-		+		+
621	-	250	+	469	=	
=		=		=		=
	+		+		=	

Magic Squares

P : 22

In a Magic Square, every row, column and diagonal all add up to make the same total.

66 (diagonal) | 66 | 66 | 66 | 66 | 66 (diagonal)

16	19	21	10	◀ 66
9	22	20	15	◀ 66
18	13	11	24	◀ 66
23	12	14	17	◀ 66

Le nombre magique est : 66

Row	Column	Diagonal
16+19+21+10=66	16+9+18+23=66	16+22+11+17=66
9+22+20+15=66	19+22+13+12=66	10+20+13+23=66
18+13+11+24=66	21+20+11+14=66	
23+12+14+17=66	10+15+24+17=66	

1.

8		11	13
19		16	10
9		6	

2.

		10	13
20		21	6
		14	
8			18

3.

10		15	4
	16	14	9
	7		
			11

4.

		13	
17			8
3			14
6		7	11

Magic Squares

5.

16			
9		20	15
18			
23	12		17

6.

9		19	12
18	13		7
15			10

7.

21	12		
15			13
			16
8	17		18

8.

6		12	
16	15		
		17	
13		7	8

Magic Squares

9.

		16	23
	19	14	
15	8	21	18

10.

	14	4	7
		17	10
15	12	6	

11.

			12
20	8		
6	18		
	21	10	14

12.

			15
21			10
	14	17	
18	19	8	

Magic Squares

13.

7		16	
	19	9	12
		22	
20			10

14.

16			14
21	8	22	
			18
	20		19

15.

	11		
23		13	
9	16		
	21	10	15

16.

10	17	19	24
21			15
			18
		14	

17.

12	5	19	
	11	13	
7		8	
9			

18.

15			9
	21		14
		10	
22	11		16

19.

	7	20	
		9	
	12	15	
16	17	6	

20.

10	3		
		11	
5		6	
7		4	13

Magic Squares

21.

			15
	16		9
	19	13	22
14		11	

22.

	20		
	17	22	
21			18
16	10	13	

23.

4	11		
		6	9
10			
	14	8	7

24.

6	13	15	20
		8	11
19		10	

25.

	14		9
17	8	22	
12	21		
10			

26.

17		7	
	10	13	
14	15	4	9

27.

	8		14
	15		
6	13	16	
	18	7	

28.

			11
10	23	21	16
19			
24			18

Magic Squares

29.

25	16		
	10	24	17
		13	
12			22

30.

12			
5	18	16	11
			20
19			13

31.

	12	14	5
8	15	9	18
			16

32.

	22		17
23	9	20	14
	19	10	

33.

13		18	
	16	21	11
		7	17
			22

34.

16			14
22	15		
			21
13	20	10	

35.

5	12		19
			10
11		20	13
			8

36.

	17		
	4	15	9
13			
8	14	5	

Magic Squares

37.

13	14		11
		19	4
			15
	17		16

38.

	13	7	10
17	4		
		11	14
	16		

39.

	16		
17		14	8
12	10		
7	13		

40.

19	10	12	5
8	17		
		9	16

41.

18	6	15	
19			10
	17		
	20	9	

42.

14	15	5	
9	4		
16	13	7	

43.

20			6
14		19	
9			
7		10	17

44.

5			
15	14		
10			
12	17	6	7

45.

17	18	12	
22			
13			19
10			20

46.

22			8
16	7		14
11		10	
			19

47.

13			
6	19	17	
15		8	21
		11	

48.

9	12		
2		13	
		4	17
	5		10

49.

18		13	16
23	10	24	
			20
		12	

50.

	10		
23	11		14
9		16	20
			17

51.

8	15		22
19	20		
21	18	12	

52.

20			
21			
		14	18
10	22	11	15

Magic Squares

53.

			18
24	10	21	
19	17		12
14			

54.

4	7		17
	13	8	
			12
11			6

55.

	18		
22	16	9	19
17		14	24

56.

10			15
	7	18	12
	14	19	
11			

57.

15	3		8
	4		7
			13
5	17		

58.

	14		7
10		11	
12	19	9	18

59.

	10		
			6
12		18	15
14	19	8	

60.

			23
20	21		
15		24	
22		13	12

Magic Squares

61.

10		15	
	13		8
		4	
12	6		19

62.

16		21	
			14
	17		20
	12	15	25

63.

	9		
22			13
8	20	15	
	23	12	

64.

9	12		22
19	18		8
		10	11

Secret Trails

Starting at the first ringed number, add numbers in a trail to reach the total for each question.

3 + 4 + 6 + 5 + 9 + 9 + 1 + 6 + 7 = 50

1.

(716)	502	300	372
151	109	947	470
283	204	961	723
478	479	348	883
		+	(4098)

2.

127	289	468	478
949	350	140	950
577	435	554	424
945	243	491	218
		+	4542

3.

167	887	109	971
980	613	578	967
709	122	144	381
953	823	526	822
		+	5290

4.

747	637	955	449
767	251	259	421
573	674	492	145
337	961	570	605
		+	5301

5.

411	461	873	807
147	675	889	511
339	328	996	669
624	611	128	602
		+	5678

6.

495	853	263	609
399	735	849	649
506	939	186	921
471	160	574	775
		+	5200

7.

511	164	949	249
700	961	165	937
528	922	263	752
949	162	464	543
		+	4930

8.

566	716	441	910
112	726	123	257
640	735	803	589
868	267	522	893
		+	4064

9.

200	964	652	840
794	892	197	671
871	812	686	897
556	877	721	478
		+	3768

10.

593	857	433	623
499	438	925	991
160	326	362	448
660	754	741	858
		+	2946

11.

961	499	890	507
772	824	343	339
240	913	437	360
(183)	858	181	210
		+	(2343)

12.

674	664	559	566
700	626	727	849
734	666	835	322
(311)	158	944	139
		+	(4583)

13.

915	322	587	716
821	133	190	384
359	524	587	731
976	467	280	337
		+	4318

14.

180	177	398	392
361	873	263	658
137	258	507	116
928	855	492	320
		+	3656

Secret Trails

15.

942	859	623	128
852	631	469	282
441	201	239	217
757	298	655	984
		+	3590

16.

977	867	741	404
654	448	424	157
783	874	682	368
431	669	195	510
		+	4957

17.

525	421	714	887
(327)	545	928	210
919	772	123	540
380	960	852	131
		+	(4282)

18.

877	625	579	181
(388)	510	298	970
169	756	787	914
110	531	144	706
		+	(3749)

Sudoku

Fill the grid so that every row, every colum and every 3x3 box contans the number 1 to 9

	4	5	8	3		1		
1	3	8	6				2	4
7	9	6	1	4	2	3		5
5			2	9	3	6	1	8
	8	9				5	3	
3		1					4	9
4	5	2	3		1	8	9	6
9	6		4		5			1
	1		9	2		4	5	3

Sudoku

1.

		5					1	
	1	4			5		6	
3		2	1		9		8	
9	4		6				2	
2	8			5	4			7
5				9	2			
4	5			1	8	6	3	
6								
	2	9		6			7	4

Sudoku

2.

	5	1	7	6	3	2	8	9
6	9	3	8	5		1	4	7
			9	1	4			3
3		8		7	9			
7		9			1	8		5
			6	3	8	7		
9			2	8	7	5	1	
	8			9	6		7	
		2			5	9		8

Sudoku

3.

	2				5			
6				7	9	1	2	
1				8		7	4	6
					2		1	
	9	1		3			8	
	3			4	8	6		9
	7	8	9	5	4			
5					7	4	9	
	4	6					5	7

4.

	3		6	2		4		
9	4	8	5		7	3		
		6		3			5	1
8	5		9	4	1		3	2
		4		8	3			5
3	9		7			1	8	
		5	3	9		8		7
		9			2			3
4		3	8	6	5	2		9

Sudoku

5.

4	8	9				2		1
		5		9			8	7
	6				8		5	9
7	4			1		8		6
5	3		9		7	1		
9	1	6		2	4		7	
8	9			4				5
	7		5		3	9	1	2

Sudoku

6.

8		4	3			1		2
		2	4					7
		7		1	2		9	4
	7			3		4	1	
4	3	9		8		2	6	5
6		1	9	4	5	7	8	
	8			2		5		6
	1		5	7		3	2	
2		5		6	3	9		1

Sudoku

7.

6				5		1		
	3			7	8	9	5	
	8	7	1					6
	6	8	7	4		2		
	1			3	6	4	9	
4	5	3			2	6	7	
	7	6		1	5	8		
2		1	3	8	7	5	6	
8	9				4			3

8.

		2	8	1	6	5		
	6	4	9	7		8	2	1
		3		5	2	6	7	9
	7	8			9		1	4
3	4		2		7		5	6
6		9					8	7
9	8	6		2			3	
1	2					4		8
	3	5	1			7		2

Sudoku

9.

			7	6	2			
8		6	1	4	3	5		
3	4				5	6	7	
2	5	8		7	9			
	6					8	5	
	3	9		8	4	7		6
6	9					2		3
	8	3		2		1	4	7
7	2		3		8	9		5

Sudoku

10.

	8			3	5	2		7
3	2	9			6	8	5	
7			8	2		6	3	9
	6	3				1		2
			3	5	2			
8		2	1		9			
			5			9	4	1
9		8	6			3		
			2	9	1		8	6

Sudoku

11.

8	9	7	5	2			6	1
2	6		7	9		3		5
	5	3	8				7	9
5	3				2	9		
	1		3	5	8		4	2
		2			6		5	
		1		3	5		9	7
9	2					5		8
		5	6			1	2	4

Sudoku

12.

		7		1		8		4
		3				6	1	5
	6					9	2	
	8	6		2		7		1
7	2					4		
	5	9			1	3	6	
	3	4	5				7	8
				4	3			6
6	7			9		2	4	3

Sudoku

13.

3	8	2	1				7	
4			8			2	5	
5		7			3	1	4	
	4		6			5	2	7
2		1		5	9		3	6
8	5			3	7			4
		4			8			1
1	3		7	9		4		5
	9		3			7	8	2

Sudoku

14.

4	7				8	5		
3	8	1		5	4			
		6	1	3	9	4		8
	4	3	6			9		5
			9	8	5	7		4
		8		4				1
8		5		9	6	1	2	7
	1	4			2		5	9
2	9	7	5	1	3			6

15.

6	5		8	2	7			
		8	5		9	6		2
	4		1					7
		7		1			9	6
4		9	2	3	8			
		5	7	9			4	
7								3
8	2	6	3	7			5	9
5	9						2	1

Sudoku

16.

		5			6		1	
	2	3	8	9				4
7		6			1			2
	6	7		3				
5			9	1				
	8	1	7				3	5
3	7					8	2	6
2	1	8		7			5	3
6		4					7	1

Sudoku

17.

7			1	4			9	3
6	3	9						1
				9	3	5		
9			8	2			3	
2	8	4		3	7			
5	7			1	6	2	8	4
	9	7				3		
	4		2		1	8	6	9
	2	6		5	9	1		7

Sudoku

18.

	5	8	2	3		6	4	7
	2	6				3		5
7			6					9
	7		4	6				8
4		1	9		2	5	7	6
		2	7		5	9		4
2		7		4		8		
6	1		5	2	8		9	
3		5	1	9				2

Key
Answer

Across Downs

1.

30 5	-	28 8	+	32 6	=	34 3
-		+		-		+
28 8	+	96 0	-	95	=	11 53
+		-		+		+
75 2	-	18 5	+	91 0	=	14 77
=		=		=		=
76 9	+	10 63	+	11 41	=	29 73

2.

31 4	-	20 0	+	74 9	=	86 3
-		+		-		+
20 0	+	33 9	-	30	=	50 9
+		-		+		+
95 4	-	18 6	+	18 3	=	95 1
=		=		=		=
10 68	+	35 3	+	90 2	=	23 23

3.

37 9	-	15 5	+	16 6	=	39 0
-		+		-		+
15 5	+	59 4	-	86	=	66 3
+		-		+		+
25 0	-	22 3	+	44 5	=	47 2
=		=		=		=
47 4	+	52 6	+	52 5	=	15 25

4.

22 2	-	38	+	30 3	=	48 7
-		+		-		+
38	+	99 5	-	52	=	98 1
+		-		+		+
45 7	-	29 1	+	54 2	=	70 8
=		=		=		=
64 1	+	74 2	+	79 3	=	21 76

5.

16 8	-	75	+	42 7	=	52 0
-		+		-		+
75	+	37 2	-	32 5	=	12 2
+		-		+		+
70 5	-	13 7	+	82 9	=	13 97
=		=		=		=
79 8	+	31 0	+	93 1	=	20 39

6.

91	-	54	+	58 6	=	62 3
-		+		-		+
54	+	42 9	-	41 8	=	65
+		-		+		+
27 1	-	65	+	36 8	=	57 4
=		=		=		=
30 8	+	41 8	+	53 6	=	12 62

7.

628	-	160	+	257	=	725
-		+		-		+
160	+	111	-	15	=	256
+		-		+		+
134	-	50	+	56	=	140
=		=		=		=
602	+	221	+	298	=	1121

8.

52	-	46	+	739	=	745
-		+		-		+
46	+	120	-	54	=	112
+		-		+		+
251	-	90	+	857	=	1018
=		=		=		=
257	+	76	+	1542	=	1875

9.

999	-	208	+	172	=	963
-		+		-		+
208	+	643	-	91	=	760
+		-		+		+
177	-	56	+	674	=	795
=		=		=		=
968	+	795	+	755	=	2518

10.

41	-	14	+	503	=	530
-		+		-		+
14	+	925	-	335	=	604
+		-		+		+
462	-	219	+	951	=	1194
=		=		=		=
489	+	720	+	1119	=	2328

11.

932	-	871	+	367	=	428
-		+		-		+
871	+	914	-	74	=	1711
+		-		+		+
525	-	217	+	35	=	343
=		=		=		=
586	+	1568	+	328	=	2482

12.

993	-	370	+	320	=	943
-		+		-		+
370	+	991	-	310	=	1051
+		-		+		+
246	-	94	+	840	=	992
=		=		=		=
869	+	1267	+	850	=	2986

13.

84 5	-	61 6	+	42 9	=	65 8
-		+		-		+
61 6	+	76 5	-	43	=	13 38
+		-		+		+
59 5	-	50 0	+	45 1	=	54 6
=		=		=		=
82 4	+	88 1	+	83 7	=	25 42

14.

94 3	-	55 0	+	71	=	46 4
-		+		-		+
55 0	+	79 2	-	45	=	12 97
+		-		+		+
52 5	-	20 6	+	58 9	=	90 8
=		=		=		=
91 8	+	11 36	+	61 5	=	26 69

15.

40 8	-	32 2	+	18 8	=	27 4
-		+		-		+
32 2	+	51 5	-	16 7	=	67 0
+		-		+		+
82 7	-	33 9	+	47 5	=	96 3
=		=		=		=
91 3	+	49 8	+	49 6	=	19 07

16.

79 4	-	11 0	+	64 9	=	13 33
-		+		-		+
11 0	+	15 6	-	13 4	=	13 2
+		-		+		+
32 0	-	11 1	+	79 5	=	10 04
=		=		=		=
10 04	+	15 5	+	13 10	=	24 69

17.

95 7	-	63 5	+	80	=	40 2
-		+		-		+
63 5	+	93 5	-	3	=	15 67
+		-		+		+
70 8	-	60 4	+	33 8	=	44 2
=		=		=		=
10 30	+	96 6	+	41 5	=	24 11

18.

95	-	88	+	97 1	=	97 8
-		+		-		+
88	+	61 6	-	28 1	=	42 3
+		-		+		+
62 1	-	25 0	+	46 9	=	84 0
=		=		=		=
62 8	+	45 4	+	11 59	=	22 41

Magic Squares

1.

8	18	11	13
19	5	16	10
14	12	17	7
9	15	6	20

50

2.

15	16	10	13
20	7	21	6
11	12	14	17
8	19	9	18

54

3.

10	13	15	4
3	16	14	9
12	7	5	18
17	6	8	11

42

4.

16	4	13	9
17	5	12	8
3	15	10	14
6	18	7	11

42

5.

16	19	21	10
9	22	20	15
18	13	11	24
23	12	14	17

66

6.

9	6	19	12
18	13	8	7
4	11	14	17
15	16	5	10

46

7.

21	12	14	7
15	6	20	13
10	19	9	16
8	17	11	18

54

8.

6	9	12	19
16	15	10	5
11	4	17	14
13	18	7	8

46

9.

10	13	16	23
20	19	14	9
15	8	21	18
17	22	11	12

62

10.

2	9	11	16
13	14	4	7
8	3	17	10
15	12	6	5

38

11.

19	7	16	12
20	8	15	11
6	18	13	17
9	21	10	14

54

12.

12	9	22	15
21	16	11	10
7	14	17	20
18	19	8	13

58

13.

7	14	16	21
18	19	9	12
13	8	22	15
20	17	11	10

58

14.

16	17	11	14
21	8	22	7
12	13	15	18
9	20	10	19

58

15.

14	11	24	17
23	18	13	12
9	16	19	22
20	21	10	15

66

16.

10	17	19	24
21	22	12	15
16	11	25	18
23	20	14	13

70

17.

12	5	19	10
18	11	13	4
7	14	8	17
9	16	6	15

46

18.

15	18	20	9
8	21	19	14
17	12	10	23
22	11	13	16

62

19.

10	7	20	13
19	14	9	8
5	12	15	18
16	17	6	11

50

20.

10	3	17	8
16	9	11	2
5	12	6	15
7	14	4	13

38

21.

17	10	24	15
23	16	18	9
12	19	13	22
14	21	11	20

66

22.

14	20	19	9
11	17	22	12
21	15	8	18
16	10	13	23

62

23.

4	11	13	18
15	16	6	9
10	5	19	12
17	14	8	7

46

24.

6	13	15	20
17	18	8	11
12	7	21	14
19	16	10	9

54

25.

23	14	16	9
17	8	22	15
12	21	11	18
10	19	13	20

62

26.

8	5	18	11
17	12	7	6
3	10	13	16
14	15	4	9

42

27.

11	8	21	14
20	15	10	9
6	13	16	19
17	18	7	12

54

28.

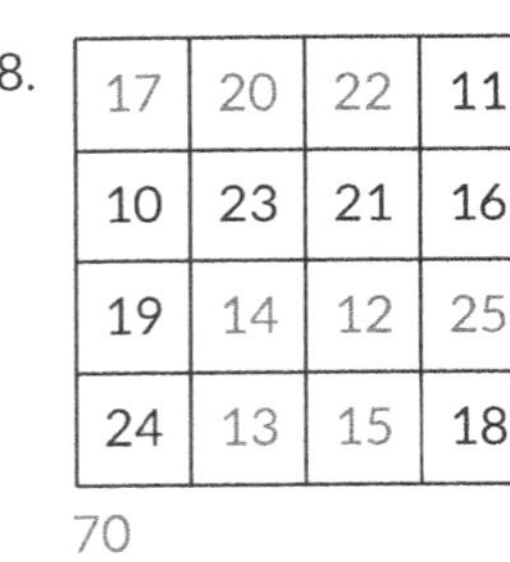

17	20	22	11
10	23	21	16
19	14	12	25
24	13	15	18

70

29.

25	16	18	11
19	10	24	17
14	23	13	20
12	21	15	22

70

30.

12	15	17	6
5	18	16	11
14	9	7	20
19	8	10	13

50

31.

13	6	20	11
19	12	14	5
8	15	9	18
10	17	7	16

50

32.

12	22	15	17
23	9	20	14
18	16	21	11
13	19	10	24

66

33.

13	19	18	8
10	16	21	11
20	14	7	17
15	9	12	22

58

34.

16	9	23	14
22	15	17	8
11	18	12	21
13	20	10	19

62

35.

5	12	14	19
16	17	7	10
11	6	20	13
18	15	9	8

50

36.

7	17	10	12
18	4	15	9
13	11	16	6
8	14	5	19

46

37.

13	14	8	11
18	5	19	4
9	10	12	15
6	17	7	16

46

38.

12	13	7	10
17	4	18	3
8	9	11	14
5	16	6	15

42

39.

6	16	9	11
17	3	14	8
12	10	15	5
7	13	4	18

42

40.

19	10	12	5
13	4	18	11
8	17	7	14
6	15	9	16

46

41.

18	6	15	11
19	7	14	10
5	17	12	16
8	20	9	13

50

42.

3	10	12	17
14	15	5	8
9	4	18	11
16	13	7	6

42

43.

20	11	13	6
14	5	19	12
9	18	8	15
7	16	10	17

50

44.

5	8	11	18
15	14	9	4
10	3	16	13
12	17	6	7

42

45.

17	18	12	15
22	9	23	8
13	14	16	19
10	21	11	20

62

46.

22	13	15	8
16	7	21	14
11	20	10	17
9	18	12	19

58

47.

13	16	18	7
6	19	17	12
15	10	8	21
20	9	11	14

54

48.

9	12	14	3
2	15	13	8
11	6	4	17
16	5	7	10

38

49.

18	19	13	16
23	10	24	9
14	15	17	20
11	22	12	21

66

50.

22	10	19	15
23	11	18	14
9	21	16	20
12	24	13	17

66

51.

8	15	17	22
19	20	10	13
14	9	23	16
21	18	12	11

62

52.

20	8	17	13
21	9	16	12
7	19	14	18
10	22	11	15

58

53.

13	23	16	18
24	10	21	15
19	17	22	12
14	20	11	25

70

54.

4	7	10	17
14	13	8	3
9	2	15	12
11	16	5	6

38

55.

15	21	20	10
12	18	23	13
22	16	9	19
17	11	14	24

66

56.

10	20	13	15
21	7	18	12
16	14	19	9
11	17	8	22

58

57.

15	3	12	8
16	4	11	7
2	14	9	13
5	17	6	10

38

58.

15	8	22	13
21	14	16	7
10	17	11	20
12	19	9	18

58

59.

7	10	13	20
17	16	11	6
12	5	18	15
14	19	8	9

50

60.

9	16	18	23
20	21	11	14
15	10	24	17
22	19	13	12

66

61.

10	16	15	5
7	13	18	8
17	11	4	14
12	6	9	19

46

62.

16	22	21	11
13	19	24	14
23	17	10	20
18	12	15	25

70

63.

21	9	18	14
22	10	17	13
8	20	15	19
11	23	12	16

62

64.

9	12	15	22
19	18	13	8
14	7	20	17
16	21	10	11

58

1.

716	502	300	372
151	109	947	470
283	204	961	723
478	479	348	883
		+	4098

2.

127	289	468	478
949	350	140	950
577	435	554	424
945	243	491	218
		+	4542

3.

167	887	109	971
980	613	578	967
709	122	144	381
953	823	526	822
		+	5290

4.

747	637	955	449
767	251	259	421
573	674	492	145
337	961	570	605
		+	5301

5.

411	461	873	807
147	675	889	511
339	328	996	669
624	611	128	602
		+	5678

6.

495	853	263	609
399	735	849	649
506	939	186	921
471	160	574	775
		+	5200

7.

511	164	949	249
700	961	165	937
528	922	263	752
949	162	464	543
		+	4930

8.

566	716	441	910
112	726	123	257
640	735	803	589
868	267	522	893
		+	4064

9.

200	964	652	840
794	892	197	671
871	812	686	897
556	877	721	478
		+	3768

10.

593	857	433	623
499	438	925	991
160	326	362	448
660	754	741	858
		+	2946

11.

961	499	890	507
772	824	343	339
240	913	437	360
183	858	181	210
		+	2343

12.

674	664	559	566
700	626	727	849
734	666	835	322
311	158	944	139
		+	4583

13.

915	322	587	716
821	133	190	384
359	524	587	731
976	467	280	337
		+	4318

14.

180	177	398	392
361	873	263	658
137	258	507	116
928	855	492	320
		+	3656

15.

942	859	623	128
852	631	469	282
441	201	239	217
757	298	655	984
		+	3590

16.

977	867	741	404
654	448	424	157
783	874	682	368
431	669	195	510
		+	4957

17.

525	421	714	887
327	545	928	210
919	772	123	540
380	960	852	131
		+	4282

18.

877	625	579	181
388	510	298	970
169	756	787	914
110	531	144	706
		+	3749

Sudoku

1.

7	9	5	2	8	6	4	1	3
8	1	4	7	3	5	2	6	9
3	6	2	1	4	9	7	8	5
9	4	3	6	7	1	5	2	8
2	8	6	3	5	4	1	9	7
5	7	1	8	9	2	3	4	6
4	5	7	9	1	8	6	3	2
6	3	8	4	2	7	9	5	1
1	2	9	5	6	3	8	7	4

2.

4	5	1	7	6	3	2	8	9
6	9	3	8	5	2	1	4	7
8	2	7	9	1	4	6	5	3
3	1	8	5	7	9	4	2	6
7	6	9	4	2	1	8	3	5
2	4	5	6	3	8	7	9	1
9	3	6	2	8	7	5	1	4
5	8	4	1	9	6	3	7	2
1	7	2	3	4	5	9	6	8

3.

7	2	4	6	1	5	9	3	8
6	8	3	4	7	9	1	2	5
1	5	9	2	8	3	7	4	6
8	6	7	5	9	2	3	1	4
4	9	1	7	3	6	5	8	2
2	3	5	1	4	8	6	7	9
3	7	8	9	5	4	2	6	1
5	1	2	8	6	7	4	9	3
9	4	6	3	2	1	8	5	7

4.

5	3	1	6	2	9	4	7	8
9	4	8	5	1	7	3	2	6
7	2	6	4	3	8	9	5	1
8	5	7	9	4	1	6	3	2
1	6	4	2	8	3	7	9	5
3	9	2	7	5	6	1	8	4
2	1	5	3	9	4	8	6	7
6	8	9	1	7	2	5	4	3
4	7	3	8	6	5	2	1	9

5.

4	8	9	7	5	6	2	3	1
3	2	5	4	9	1	6	8	7
1	6	7	2	3	8	4	5	9
7	4	2	3	1	5	8	9	6
5	3	8	9	6	7	1	2	4
9	1	6	8	2	4	5	7	3
8	9	3	1	4	2	7	6	5
2	5	1	6	7	9	3	4	8
6	7	4	5	8	3	9	1	2

6.

8	6	4	3	9	7	1	5	2
1	9	2	4	5	8	6	3	7
3	5	7	6	1	2	8	9	4
5	7	8	2	3	6	4	1	9
4	3	9	7	8	1	2	6	5
6	2	1	9	4	5	7	8	3
7	8	3	1	2	9	5	4	6
9	1	6	5	7	4	3	2	8
2	4	5	8	6	3	9	7	1

7.

6	2	9	4	5	3	1	8	7
1	3	4	6	7	8	9	5	2
5	8	7	1	2	9	3	4	6
9	6	8	7	4	1	2	3	5
7	1	2	5	3	6	4	9	8
4	5	3	8	9	2	6	7	1
3	7	6	9	1	5	8	2	4
2	4	1	3	8	7	5	6	9
8	9	5	2	6	4	7	1	3

8.

7	9	2	8	1	6	5	4	3
5	6	4	9	7	3	8	2	1
8	1	3	4	5	2	6	7	9
2	7	8	5	6	9	3	1	4
3	4	1	2	8	7	9	5	6
6	5	9	3	4	1	2	8	7
9	8	6	7	2	4	1	3	5
1	2	7	6	3	5	4	9	8
4	3	5	1	9	8	7	6	2

9.

9	1	5	7	6	2	4	3	8
8	7	6	1	4	3	5	9	2
3	4	2	8	9	5	6	7	1
2	5	8	6	7	9	3	1	4
4	6	7	2	3	1	8	5	9
1	3	9	5	8	4	7	2	6
6	9	1	4	5	7	2	8	3
5	8	3	9	2	6	1	4	7
7	2	4	3	1	8	9	6	5

10.

6	8	4	9	3	5	2	1	7
3	2	9	7	1	6	8	5	4
7	5	1	8	2	4	6	3	9
5	6	3	4	7	8	1	9	2
1	9	7	3	5	2	4	6	8
8	4	2	1	6	9	5	7	3
2	7	6	5	8	3	9	4	1
9	1	8	6	4	7	3	2	5
4	3	5	2	9	1	7	8	6

11.

8	9	7	5	2	3	4	6	1
2	6	4	7	9	1	3	8	5
1	5	3	8	6	4	2	7	9
5	3	8	4	7	2	9	1	6
6	1	9	3	5	8	7	4	2
7	4	2	9	1	6	8	5	3
4	8	1	2	3	5	6	9	7
9	2	6	1	4	7	5	3	8
3	7	5	6	8	9	1	2	4

12.

5	9	7	2	1	6	8	3	4
2	4	3	9	8	7	6	1	5
1	6	8	3	5	4	9	2	7
3	8	6	4	2	9	7	5	1
7	2	1	6	3	5	4	8	9
4	5	9	8	7	1	3	6	2
9	3	4	5	6	2	1	7	8
8	1	2	7	4	3	5	9	6
6	7	5	1	9	8	2	4	3

13.

3	8	2	1	4	5	6	7	9
4	1	9	8	7	6	2	5	3
5	6	7	9	2	3	1	4	8
9	4	3	6	8	1	5	2	7
2	7	1	4	5	9	8	3	6
8	5	6	2	3	7	9	1	4
7	2	4	5	6	8	3	9	1
1	3	8	7	9	2	4	6	5
6	9	5	3	1	4	7	8	2

14.

4	7	9	2	6	8	5	1	3
3	8	1	7	5	4	6	9	2
5	2	6	1	3	9	4	7	8
7	4	3	6	2	1	9	8	5
1	6	2	9	8	5	7	3	4
9	5	8	3	4	7	2	6	1
8	3	5	4	9	6	1	2	7
6	1	4	8	7	2	3	5	9
2	9	7	5	1	3	8	4	6

15.

6	5	1	8	2	7	9	3	4
3	7	8	5	4	9	6	1	2
9	4	2	1	6	3	5	8	7
2	8	7	4	1	5	3	9	6
4	6	9	2	3	8	1	7	5
1	3	5	7	9	6	2	4	8
7	1	4	9	5	2	8	6	3
8	2	6	3	7	1	4	5	9
5	9	3	6	8	4	7	2	1

16.

8	4	5	3	2	6	7	1	9
1	2	3	8	9	7	5	6	4
7	9	6	4	5	1	3	8	2
4	6	7	5	3	2	1	9	8
5	3	2	9	1	8	6	4	7
9	8	1	7	6	4	2	3	5
3	7	9	1	4	5	8	2	6
2	1	8	6	7	9	4	5	3
6	5	4	2	8	3	9	7	1

17.

7	5	8	1	4	2	6	9	3
6	3	9	7	8	5	4	2	1
4	1	2	6	9	3	5	7	8
9	6	1	8	2	4	7	3	5
2	8	4	5	3	7	9	1	6
5	7	3	9	1	6	2	8	4
1	9	7	4	6	8	3	5	2
3	4	5	2	7	1	8	6	9
8	2	6	3	5	9	1	4	7

18.

1	5	8	2	3	9	6	4	7
9	2	6	8	7	4	3	1	5
7	4	3	6	5	1	2	8	9
5	7	9	4	6	3	1	2	8
4	3	1	9	8	2	5	7	6
8	6	2	7	1	5	9	3	4
2	9	7	3	4	6	8	5	1
6	1	4	5	2	8	7	9	3
3	8	5	1	9	7	4	6	2

Made in United States
North Haven, CT
24 October 2022

25863834R00050